To Dear Little Lucy
on the happy day
of your
Baptism
July 11th 1976.

Love From Auntie Lulu M.

No Ordinary Child

With words by Peggy Blakeley & drawings by Edith Witt · Adam and Charles Black · London

Folk hurried along from everywhere
when they heard the commotion
in the square.

Farmers and shepherds
came down from the hills,
housewives with pitchers
on their way to the well
stopped
to hear the news
the king's men had to tell.

And Joseph the carpenter was there
so he
like the rest of them
listened well.

Then full of excitement
he hurried home
to explain to Mary
about the journey they'd have to make.

And they talked and planned
as people do
of the things they'd need to pack and take.

Mary
thought they should wrap up warm
against the cold.
Joseph felt adventurous and very bold
to be travelling back to Bethlehem
so far away.
But he knew he'd have his tax to pay.

They were up very early
before it was light.
Their little donkey was led from his stall
clip-clop over the stones
while still up above them the stars shone bright.

Through the quiet streets
and out of the town,
on winding paths up hill and down.
Up hill and down by night and day
they journeyed.
But Mary
grew weary on the way.

But at last they came to Bethlehem town
tired and ready to rest,
and they both looked forward as anyone would
to some good hot food
and a chance to sleep in a comfortable bed
and a place for their donkey to lay himself down.

But "I've no room," the innkeeper said,
"People are packed in everywhere,
I haven't got an inch to spare."

The he looked again at Mary
so tired and so sad.
"I tell you what," he suddenly said.
"If you'll come with me to my backyard I've a stable there.
The floors are stone and very hard
but there's plenty of hay
and the animals will keep you warm
so you'll come to no harm."

Thankfully
Mary and Joseph
walked through the cobbled yard at the back of the inn
and all the while
the innkeeper talked
of the crowds who had come to Bethlehem.

It was warm in the stable
after the cold night air.
Joseph
hung the lantern high
and spread some blankets for Mary's bed.
Then
he watered and fed the little donkey
while the cattle stirred restlessly in the hay.

"And now, good night," the innkeeper called
and he shut the door and went away.

And there
in that bare and lonely place
far away from home
Mary's baby was born.

She wrapped him up tight
to keep out the cold as best she could,
then
she gave him to Joseph to hold
while they looked around
for something to make him a bed.

"We'll lay him in the manger
on some fresh clean hay,
it will make a fine cradle,"
Joseph said.

Now out on a hillside
huddled round their dying fire and half asleep
some shepherds
were watching by their restless sheep.

Suddenly
they were startled
by a vivid golden light
that shone around them
and seemed to set the midnight sky alight.

And a clear high voice
which echoed in the hills
told them not to be afraid of anything
but to follow the largest star
which would lead them into Bethlehem
and to a stable
where they would be the first
to see a new-born king.

The shepherds
now more excited than afraid
decided among themselves
that this was a very special sign
and it must be obeyed.

And they followed
the gleaming, glittering star
which seemed to beckon
and to light
a pathway for them through the night.

Up and down
the stony tracks they ran
until at last
they came to Bethlehem.

Three very grand and splendid kings
also followed that guiding star—
Melchior
Caspar
and Balthazaar.

They came from the East
a great cavalcade of horses and camels
travelling
through the heat of the day and cold of the night
until at last they came in sight
of Bethlehem.

Richly dressed in silk and fur
they carried gifts for a baby king,
precious gifts
of gold
and frankincense
and myrrh.

Mary
who had not expected visitors
made the shepherds welcome when they came.
She said her baby's name
was Jesus
and listened to them
when they told of the voice
and the strange bright light
which had led them through the night
to the stable.

And then from outside
came a great fuss and noise.
The stable door was opened wide
and into that quiet, homely place
strode the three kings
who bowed down low to the little baby
where he lay
sleeping so softly in the hay.

At last
everyone went away.

First the shepherds
who couldn't wait to tell
all that they had heard and seen that day.

Then the three great kings
thinking deep, wise thoughts
who left by the manger
the gifts they'd brought.

Mary
glad to have a rest at the end of the day
lay
in the warm hay
listening to the night sounds.

To the cattle's comfortable shuffle,
to the creak of the lantern
swinging in the draught
as the wind outside grew wild.

And she pondered in her heart
about her baby,
knowing now
that he must be
no ordinary child.